# ANCIENT INDIA

BY SARA GREEN

BELLWETHER MEDIA · MINNEAPOLIS, MN

**Blastoff! Discovery** launches a new mission: reading to learn. Filled with facts and features, each book offers you an exciting new world to explore!

This edition first published in 2020 by Bellwether Media, Inc.

No part of this publication may be reproduced in whole or in part without written permission of the publisher.
For information regarding permission, write to Bellwether Media, Inc., Attention: Permissions Department,
6012 Blue Circle Drive, Minnetonka, MN 55343.

Library of Congress Cataloging-in-Publication Data

Names: Green, Sara, 1964- author.
Title: Ancient India / By Sara Green.
Description: Minneapolis, MN : Bellwether Media, Inc., 2020. |
    Series: Blastoff! Discovery: Ancient Civilizations |
    Includes bibliographical references and index. |
    Audience: Ages 7-13 | Audience: Grades 4-6 |
    Summary: "Engaging images accompany information about
    ancient India. The combination of high-interest subject matter
    and narrative text is intended for students in grades 3 through 8"
    – Provided by publisher.
Identifiers: LCCN 2019036008 (print) | LCCN 2019036009
    (ebook) | ISBN 9781644871775 (library binding) |
    ISBN 9781618918611 (paperback) | ISBN 9781618918536
    (ebook)
Subjects: LCSH: India–Civilization–Juvenile literature. |
    India–History–Juvenile literature. | India–Social life and
    customs–Juvenile literature.
Classification: LCC DS421 .G76 2020 (print) | LCC DS421 (ebook)
    | DDC 934–dc23
LC record available at https://lccn.loc.gov/2019036008
LC ebook record available at https://lccn.loc.gov/2019036009

Editor: Kate Moening      Designer: Jeffrey Kollock

Printed in the United States of America, North Mankato, MN.

# TABLE OF CONTENTS

# MARKETS AND MUSIC

MODERN INDIAN MARKETPLACE

It is a busy day at the market in ancient India! A girl and her mother walk through the stalls in the Gupta city of Mathura. They buy rice, lentils, and grapes. They skip the meat seller, though. Their Buddhist family eats a **vegetarian** diet.

VEENA PERFORMANCE

The girl is especially excited this morning. Later, her family will attend a musical performance. She hopes to hear a musician playing a stringed instrument called a *veena*. It is her favorite!

# WHO WERE THE ANCIENT INDIANS?

INDUS RIVER IN
LADAKH, INDIA

Ancient India was a period that lasted from around 1500 BCE to 550 CE. Several civilizations ruled the region over time. The largest, the Mauryan Empire, extended over what is now India, Pakistan, Nepal, and Bangladesh. Its population may have reached 30 million people.

India's name comes from the Indus River. Early Indian settlers used the word *sindhu* for the waterway. This means "river" in Sanskrit. In the 300s BCE, Greeks began saying Indus instead.

## MAURYAN EMPIRE 321-185 BCE

KEY    ■ Mauryan Empire

INDUS RIVER

GANGES RIVER

N W E S

Around 1500 BCE, a group called the Aryans arrived in the Indus Valley. This was the beginning of India's Vedic period. Early Aryans were **nomads** from central Asia. Along the Indus and Ganges Rivers, they became farmers! The area had rich soil to farm. **Natural resources** such as iron helped new villages gain wealth. In time, the villages grew into India's first kingdoms.

# ⌐IRON⌐

India's Iron Age began during the Vedic period. The Iron Age brought important changes in farming and warfare. Researchers have uncovered iron pieces in India that date to around 1300 BCE!

## HOW IRON HELPED THE ANCIENT INDIAN CIVILIZATION GROW

☑ iron tools helped cut down forests quickly for farming

☑ iron farm tools allowed farmers to till tougher soil

☑ trading iron helped the civilization gain other goods and build wealth

☑ iron pillars and other structures lasted centuries

☑ iron weapons were stronger and more powerful than bronze or stone

**THINK ABOUT IT**

Why would the Aryans change their lifestyle when they arrived at the Indus and Ganges Rivers?

Later, the Mauryan **dynasty** united the kingdoms into one empire. The empire used military force to grow even larger.

Ancient India is best remembered for its advances during the Gupta Empire. The Guptas made important progress in math, science, **astronomy**, medicine, and writing. The numbers used today come from the Gupta period. The Guptas even invented chess!

In the late 400s CE, a man named Aryabhata studied math and astronomy. He invented the **decimal system** we still use today. He was also the first person to argue that Earth is round!

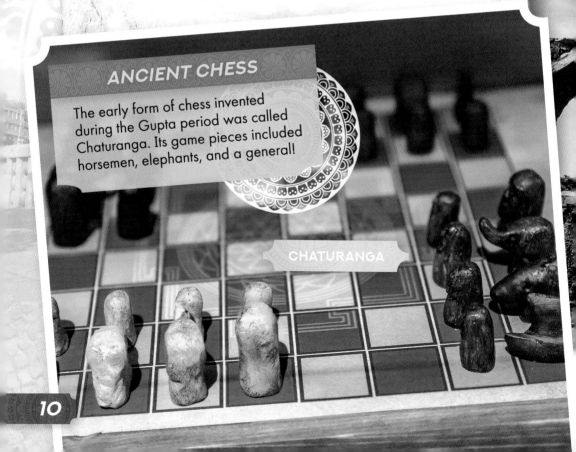

### ANCIENT CHESS

The early form of chess invented during the Gupta period was called Chaturanga. Its game pieces included horsemen, elephants, and a general!

CHATURANGA

IRON PILLAR IN DELHI, INDIA

# HOW THE ANCIENT INDIANS RULED

**ANCIENT INDIA SURRENDERS TO MACEDONIAN ARMY**

Ancient India's government changed with each ruling civilization. Chiefs called *rajas* led Aryan tribes. Rajas protected their people and cattle from enemies.

By around 650 BCE, Aryan tribes had formed sixteen kingdoms. But the foreign Persian civilization **invaded** the area in 550 BCE. Two centuries later, Macedonia's Alexander the Great took control. But Alexander only stayed in India for two years. Soon after he left, the Mauryan Empire took control.

# PERIODS OF ANCIENT INDIA

## GENDER EQUALITY

- boys and girls attended school
- women had similar rights to men

## KNOWN FOR

- the Vedas
- early Hinduism and Buddhism
- early caste system

## VEDIC PERIOD
### AROUND 1500 TO 500 BCE

## GOVERNMENT

- rajas chosen by members of Aryan tribes

## SOCIAL CLASS
- varnas

## GENDER EQUALITY

- only boys attended school
- women could have jobs and own property

## KNOWN FOR

- powerful army
- strong central government
- one of world's largest empires

## MAURYAN EMPIRE
### AROUND 321 BCE TO 185 BCE

## GOVERNMENT

- Mauryan-born kings

## SOCIAL CLASS
- caste system

## KNOWN FOR

- invention of decimals and numbers
- discovery that Earth is round and circles the sun

## GENDER EQUALITY

- only boys attended school
- women could not own property

## GUPTA EMPIRE
### AROUND 320 TO 550 CE

## GOVERNMENT

- Gupta-born kings

## SOCIAL CLASS
- caste system

ASHOKA THE GREAT, AN EMPEROR OF THE MAURYAN EMPIRE

India's Mauryan Empire began with Chandragupta Maurya. Around 321 BCE, he united India with his powerful army. The new emperor created a strong government. He built great wealth through war and trade. The Mauryan Empire became one of the largest in the world!

CHAUKHANDI STUPA IN SARNATH, INDIA

## THE MIGHTY MAURYANS

The Mauryan army was the largest military force of its time. It included 600,000 foot soldiers and 9,000 military elephants!

After the Mauryan dynasty fell in 185 BCE, small kingdoms ruled once more. But around 320 CE, a man named Chandragupta I claimed power. His military might helped him found the Gupta dynasty. The Gupta Empire was a peaceful time. It reigned until ancient India's end.

# DAILY LIFE

Society in India's ancient empires was largely based on daily life during the Vedic period. Early Aryans were largely **egalitarian**. But as they settled onto farms, Aryans organized people into four groups. They called these groups *varnas*. Each varna had its own jobs and rules. Aryans believed varnas led to a peaceful, orderly society. They thought clear rules brought people freedom, or *moksha*.

After the Vedic period, varnas became known as **castes**. People were born into their caste. They could not change castes or marry outside of their own. The caste system impacts Indian life even today.

## CASTES OF INDIA

**BRAHMANA**
PRIESTS AND TEACHERS

**KSHATRIYA**
WARRIORS AND NOBLES

**VAISHYA**
TRADERS, ARTISANS, AND FARMERS

**SHUDRA**
LABORERS AND SERVANTS

Education changed over time, too. During the Vedic period, both boys and girls went to school. At age 5, boys went to live at school with their teacher, called the *guru*. The boys studied math, science, writing, and other subjects. Girls studied at home. Many grew up to be community leaders, artists, or priestesses.

After the Vedic period, boys learned different skills based on their caste. But women's **status** had fallen. Women could no longer take part in many public activities. Most girls had to stay home to care for children and do chores.

VEDIC STUDENTS PRAYING

**THINK ABOUT IT**

What could have led to the loss of women's rights in ancient India?

MODERN GURU

TRADITIONAL
BAMBOO HOMES

Family was important in ancient India. Usually, the eldest male was the head of the household. Most people lived in one-room huts made of wood or bamboo. Even palaces were made of wood!

BARLEY

**THINK ABOUT IT**

Why might some religions encourage a vegetarian diet?

LENTILS

GHEE

Ancient Indians ate a lot of vegetables and grains. Lentils, rice, barley, and beans were **staples**. People also ate bread, fruits, and a special butter called *ghee*. Some ate pigs, chickens, or goats. But religions such as Buddhism encouraged people to eat a vegetarian diet.

# BELIEFS AND CULTURE

GREAT STATUE OF BUDDHA
IN BODH GAYA, INDIA

Several important religions began in ancient India. The Aryans were deeply religious. The Vedic period is named after their sacred books called the Vedas. The books held songs, prayers, and **rituals**. They taught people to respect all living things. The Vedas' teachings formed the beginning of the Hindu religion.

Around 560 BCE, a man named Siddhartha Gautama was born a prince in what is now Nepal. He founded a religion called Buddhism. Buddhism taught people to live in the present moment to find peace and truth. Today, Hinduism and Buddhism are among the largest religions in the world.

# HINDUISM AND BUDDHISM

## HINDUISM

**FOUNDER** ∎ none

**IMPORTANT TEXTS**
- the Vedas
- Bhagavad Gita
- Upanishads

**ORIGIN** ∎ as early as 2000 BCE

**AFTERLIFE**
- rebirth based on past actions
- living morally leads to heavenly bliss

**GODS** ∎ many

**BELIEFS**
- everything is part of an all-powerful force
- people have duties called *dharma* to fulfill

## BUDDHISM

**FOUNDER** ∎ Siddhartha Gautama, the Buddha

**ORIGIN** ∎ around 500 BCE

**IMPORTANT TEXTS**
- Tripitaka

**AFTERLIFE**
- rebirth based on past actions
- finding truth leads to heavenly bliss

**GODS** ∎ none; people follow their own journey

**BELIEFS**
- truth and peace are found by living in the present
- wanting things causes suffering

Much of ancient Indian art was religious. During the Gupta Empire, beautiful Hindu temples were built across the country. These were meant as homes for the gods. Mauryan and Gupta artists painted caves with scenes of the Buddha's life. Many of these are still there!

BUDDHIST ART, AJANTA CAVES

# SANSKRIT AND ENGLISH

Sanskrit is rarely spoken today. It is mainly used by Hindu priests. But it has a lot in common with European languages, including Greek, Latin, and English.
See if any of these Sanskrit words sound familiar!

| SANSKRIT | ENGLISH |
|---|---|
| gau | cow |
| kaal | calendar |
| lubh | love |
| matr | mother, maternal |
| naame | name |

Writing became another important art form. Early in ancient India, Sanskrit was mostly used for trade records. But later Vedic writers created some of the first **epic poems**. The Guptas preserved these poems and saw new poetry and plays develop.

# THE FALL OF ANCIENT INDIA

BATTLE BETWEEN HUNS AND INDIA

The Gupta Empire began to fall in the late 400s CE.
Weak leadership shook the empire's safety and economy.
Some regions **rebelled** and broke away from Gupta control.

A group called the Huns also attacked from central Asia. These fierce warriors first entered India around 450 CE. By 500, the Huns had captured much of the northwest empire. The Gupta Empire finally ended around 550 CE. It divided into independent kingdoms once more. Centuries would pass before India united again.

# INDIA TIMELINE

**AROUND 321 BCE**
Chandragupta Maurya forms the Mauryan Empire

**AROUND 320 CE**
Chandragupta I founds the Gupta Empire

**AROUND 1500 BCE**
Aryans move into India and the Vedic period begins

**550 CE**
the Gupta Empire falls

**550 BCE**
Persia invades India and the Vedic period ends 30 years later

**AROUND 1000 BCE**
the four castes are created

Today, India is a large country of more than 1 billion people. Many Indians continue practices of their **ancestors**. Hinduism is India's largest religion. The caste system also still affects life for many people.

Ancient India also changed life around the world. Billions of people still use India's numbers and decimals. Buddhism is becoming more popular in Europe and North America. Ancient India's **legacy** lives on in modern India and across the globe!

### AHIMSA

Hinduism and Buddhism teach non-violence, or *ahimsa*. The Indian leader Mahatma Gandhi and civil rights leader Martin Luther King, Jr. both practiced non-violence.

# GLOSSARY

**ancestors**—relatives who lived long ago

**astronomy**—the study of objects beyond Earth, such as planets and stars

**castes**—social classes determined by a person's birth and the jobs of their family members

**decimal system**—a number system based on 10; the decimal system uses ten digits from 0 to 9 to form all possible numbers.

**dynasty**—a line of rulers that come from the same family

**egalitarian**—believing that all people are equal to one another and have equal rights

**epic poems**—long poems that tell stories of great heroes

**invaded**—entered an area to take it over or to steal from it

**legacy**—anything that is passed down from people who lived in the past

**natural resources**—things found in nature that can be used by people

**nomads**—people who have no fixed home but wander from place to place

**rebelled**—fought to change the government of a country or region, often through protests or violence

**rituals**—religious ceremonies or practices

**staples**—widely used foods or other items

**status**—the social position or rank of a person

**vegetarian**—related to a diet that excludes meat

# TO LEARN MORE

## AT THE LIBRARY

Faust, Daniel R. *Ancient India*. New York, N.Y.: Gareth Stevens Publishing, 2019.

Johnson, Anne E. *Exploring Ancient India*. Mankato, Minn.: 12 Story Library, 2018.

Nichols, Susan. *The Culture of Ancient India*. New York, N.Y.: Rosen Publishing, 2017.

## ON THE WEB

**FACTSURFER**

Factsurfer.com gives you a safe, fun way to find more information.

1. Go to www.factsurfer.com.

2. Enter "ancient India" into the search box and click Q.

3. Select your book cover to see a list of related web sites.

# INDEX